MW00965606

Presented to:

_____

From:

Toledo Baptist Temple
Billy V. Bartlett, Pastor

_____

Date:

June 17, 2001

_____

THE GREATEST FATHER WHO EVER LIVED

Daniel R. Johnson

Providence
PUBLICATIONS

P.O. Box 882 • Kokomo, IN 46903-0882

The truths in this book surrounding the life and ministry of God are factual. All other characters are fictional.

THE GREATEST FATHER WHO EVER LIVED

published by Providence Publications

© 2001 by Daniel R. Johnson

International Standard Book Number: 0-9671383-2-9

Book and cover design by James W. Johnson

Printed in the United States of America

Scripture quotations are from the King James Version (KJV).

ALL RIGHTS RESERVED.

No part of this book may be reproduced or transmitted in any form or by any means—electronic, mechanical, photocopying, recording, or otherwise—without prior written permission from Providence Publications.

For information:
PROVIDENCE PUBLICATIONS
P.O. Box 882 • Kokomo, IN 46903-0882

With gratitude to . . .
the one whose
constant love,
rich wisdom,
and gentle leadership
has shaped my life
and given me an
inspiring example
to follow—
my father.

IT BEGAN AS an ordinary business trip, but by the time it was over it had begun to change my life. I was eager to get home because I had promised to go with my wife to her doctor's appointment late that afternoon. Jenny was pregnant with our first child. When I arrived at the Seattle airport early in the morning, I needed everything to run smoothly in order to make it home on time.

I hadn't been at the airport very long when I realized that "running smoothly" would not be the theme of the morning. My flight, scheduled to leave at 7:20 A.M., was cancelled due to fog. The next flight was overbooked, and so I missed it too. At that point, my patience was beginning to wear thin.

After calling home and telling Jenny that she would have to go to her appointment without me—then waiting in the airport for nearly seven hours—I finally boarded a plane. The one bright spot in the midst of my otherwise frustrating day was that the airline had bumped me up to first class.

In spite of the long delay, it was nice to finally be on the plane and ready to leave. It was especially nice to be seated in the first class section—something that was new to me. As the plane was filling up, no one sat down beside me. For a while it looked as if I would have both seats to myself for the flight home! At the last minute though a man walked through the door and sat down next to me.

Once settled in his seat, he reached out to shake my hand and introduce himself. He must have been at least six-feet-six, and he had the biggest hands I had ever seen! He told me his name was Alan; I said my name was Mike. I then proceeded to pull out a file folder of work that I really needed to finish.

I had barely begun my work when another passenger walked up to Alan and asked him for his autograph. I almost dropped my file folder. Who was this famous person sitting next to me? Why didn't I recognize him? I overheard enough of their conversation to discover that Alan used to play professional football.

After the other passenger returned to his seat, I closed my folder and asked Alan about his football career. He told me he had played defensive end for nine seasons with two different teams from 1972–1981. He retired after suffering a serious knee injury. Like me, he was on his way home to Phoenix. He was hoping to make it home in time for his grandson's birthday party scheduled for later that evening.

After I told him about my airport ordeal and about missing the doctor's appointment, he showed me a picture of his family. The picture included his wife, their four children and two grandchildren. Noticing what a proud father and grandfather he was, I said, "Your kids must have been pretty lucky to have had a professional football player for a dad." He kind of laughed and said it had both its advantages and its disadvantages. Playing professional football had created a lot of nice opportunities, but it had also produced its fair share of challenges.

Alan then innocently said something that changed the course of our conversation—and eventually my life. He said, "It doesn't matter what you do for a living; kids just want a dad to love them and spend time with them. Didn't you feel that way about your dad?"

Even though I'm not accustomed to personal conversations with people I meet on airplanes, I went ahead and told Alan that his question was hard for me answer. The question was hard because my dad had died in an automobile accident when I was only four years old.

My mom had raised me by herself, which was not only tough on me while growing up, but had also left me a little less than confident about becoming a father. I didn't know what to do or what not to do.

My circumstances struck a chord with Alan. He went on to tell me that his parents were divorced when he was just seven years old, so he could understand how I felt, becoming a dad without having a father.

What he then told me not only included a few good football stories but it also began to transform the way I viewed fatherhood. His story touched me so deeply I eventually convinced him to write it down. Here's what he wrote:

Today, many people look at me and see the excitement of my football career and even the success of my business investments. What they don't see is the fact that my life started a long way from success.

Life began for me in Detroit, Michigan, where I was born in the fall of 1950. Dad worked at one of the big auto plants, while Mom stayed at home. As I got older, my mom would tell me that both she and Dad were young and immature when they decided to get married. She said they thought they were in love, but the longer they were together, the further they drifted apart.

I don't remember many details about my parents' relationship, other than the memory of it being full of conflict. I can vaguely recall some of the fights, and I'll never forget the day when my dad left and never came back. I was in the first grade and I can still replay the events of that day in my mind.

Dad cleared all of his stuff out of the house, and then before he left, he gave me a hug and told me I would have to be the man of the house. Being only seven years old, I had no idea what he meant. He told me the problems were between Mom and him, but it sure felt like he was leaving me just as much as he was leaving Mom. While I sat on the front step with tears coming down my cheeks, I watched his car get smaller and smaller and smaller as he drove away.

Even before the divorce, my relationship with my dad was fairly distant but afterwards it was non-existent. He started a new life that didn't include me.

What made it especially hard was that back in the '50s, divorce was rather rare compared to today. I was the only kid in my class at school who came from a "broken" home. Because of what I've gone through, I've come to believe that no child should have to grow up without a dad!

With my dad gone, Mom had to

get a job. She worked in a department store for a while and then she got a job at a small factory where she worked for many years. In spite of having the odds stacked against her, my mom was wonderful. She loved me, tried to give me as much attention as she could, and she tried to keep me out of trouble, which was at times a big challenge.

My life began to move in a positive direction when I was in junior high. That was when I first tasted what would later bring great satisfaction into my life. In seventh grade, I met Mark, who introduced me to football. Even though I was the biggest kid in my class, it wasn't until I met Mark that I thought about playing football.

Mark had gone to a different

elementary school than I did, but when we met in junior high we quickly developed an awesome friendship. Our friendship was probably a surprise to most because in many ways Mark and I were as different as day and night! Mark was a smart, religious kid from a big family. As for me, I struggled with grades, never went to church, and I lived alone with my mom. What connected us was football, or at least that was our first connection.

Shortly after I met Mark, I discovered that his dad was Jack Miller. Jack Miller was the varsity football coach at the high school that both of us would later attend. Before meeting Mark, I barely knew anything about football. That quickly changed! We played pick-up games in Mark's backyard, in a league during junior high, and eventually, we played for Mark's dad in high school.

Mark's dad (or, "Coach," as I would end up calling him) taught me every element of the game. He spent hours teaching me key skills, tactics, and helping me to develop an instinct for the game. Over the next six years, Coach Miller dramatically affected my ability to play football, but more importantly, he deeply influenced my life. He inspired me to use all my abilities and achieve my fullest potential.

In many ways, Coach became the father I always wanted but never had. Coach and his wife, Nancy, were the first ones who showed me what a loving marriage was supposed to look like, and how a father was supposed to treat his children.

The Millers didn't take the place of my mom, but when she was working, she was happy that I had a solid "home away from home." During some weeks I think I ate more meals at their house than at my own.

A highlight each year was when they invited me to go with them to a little cabin they owned in northern Michigan. Coach had built most of it himself. It wasn't fancy, but it was situated in an absolutely beautiful location not far from Lake Michigan. While we were there, the problems and pressures that surrounded my life at home seemed millions of miles away!

While I was in high school, I

spent more and more time at Mark's home. I also began to excel at football. Mark and I played on both the offensive and defensive teams. I played tight end and defensive end while Mark played fullback and linebacker. We were both named to the All-State football team during our senior year. It was more fun than words can describe!

When it came time for us to graduate from high school, it was 1968. That was not the best year to be graduating from high school because it was at the height of the Vietnam War. Mark and I both knew that if we didn't get scholarships to play football, we would probably end up somewhere in southeast Asia. Although we were willing to go almost anywhere in order to play, we wanted to go to the same school, so when we each got an offer to play for the same university—we jumped at the chance.

I was the first one in our family to ever go to college, which made my mom incredibly proud. Coach was equally proud. When I found out the scholarship had come through, I went straight to Coach's office with the letter. I was screaming and yelling with excitement and as soon as he saw it, he joined in. I'll be forever grateful to Coach for preparing and motivating me to succeed.

Mark and I moved into the dorm in August of '68. Those were pretty wild times on most college campuses—including ours. There were protests against the war, drugs were commonly available, parties were constant, and I can't remember many moments when music wasn't blaring. All of that was especially tough for Mark, because he was still pretty serious about his spirituality.

Part of what helped Mark endure the pressure of those days was that just about every week he got a note in the mail from his dad. They weren't long letters but just a paragraph or two that mentioned how things were going at home. Each note always included a word of encouragement or inspiration.

I think Mark looked forward to the notes from his dad as much as he did to our games each Saturday. The notes, coupled with Mark's own resolve, kept him away from the wild side of college life. I wasn't quite so disciplined.

While we regularly attended our classes, our primary focus was football. Mark was able to make the starting line-up by the end of our freshman year. To this day, I have never known anyone with greater natural athletic ability than Mark Miller! I still think he was the best linebacker with whom I have ever played. He was quick, strong, and had an uncanny ability to sense what the offense was about to do. There was no doubt in anyone's mind that Mark was headed toward a professional football career. By the end of our sophomore season I had also made the starting line-up.

During the summers, since my mom was still working long hours,

I spent more time at Mark's house than my own.

One day while at the Miller's cabin, we took their sailboat out on Lake Michigan, hoping for a calm and relaxing day. We made the mistake of not checking the weather report, so we didn't realize that a storm was heading in our direction. Early on it wasn't too bad, especially since Mark had a contagious kind of confidence. Since I really didn't know much about sailboats, I just did what Mark and Coach told me to do.

As we cruised through the water, we talked about all kinds of things, but mostly about life and football. With so many guys our age fighting in the distant jungles of South Vietnam, Mark and I felt incredibly fortunate to be in the situation we were in—playing college football. As we talked, the weather conditions continued to deteriorate. I knew it was getting bad when Coach insisted that we needed to get back to the dock.

As Mark worked the sails, he told me to move to the other side of the boat. The winds were so strong that we needed as much weight as possible on that side of the boat in order to keep us from capsizing. With all three of us on the same side of the boat and the wind gusting, the boat seemed to be flying through the water.

That's when everything started to go horribly wrong. We hit a huge wave, and even though I thought I was hanging on, my grip wasn't tight enough, and I was thrown backward into the water. I was wearing a life jacket, but the roughness of the water, and the fact that I wasn't a strong swimmer, scared me like never before. All I could think of was trying to keep my head above the surface. I was trying to breathe and hoping to survive. It's hard to describe what it feels like when you honestly wonder whether or not you're about to die!

Coach and Mark frantically worked the sails and somehow managed to bring the boat fairly close to me. They threw a lifesaving ring out to me several times, but the wind and the waves were so strong that it never got close enough for me to reach it. I was starting to panic when Mark dove into the water. Holding onto the lifesaving ring, he fought through the water to reach me.

When he got to me, Mark tried to hold my head above the water, while Coach pulled the rope attached to the ring. I was so exhausted from fighting the waves that I didn't have enough strength to pull myself into the boat. With Coach steadily pulling the rope, I finally made it back on board. I remember lying there shivering, trying to recover, and unsure of what to do next.

In the excitement of the moment, I mistakenly had brought the lifesaving ring—and its rope—with me into the boat. Unfortunately, that left Mark in the water with nothing to hold onto. I was stunned when Coach reached over the side and pulled Mark into the boat. Mark was a big guy, yet Coach lifted him up as if he were a small child!

In an instant, I saw the closeness of their relationship as I had never seen it before. They had what I always wanted but had never experienced with my own dad. Not only were they father and son, but close friends as well.

The connection between the three of us deepened dramatically that day. Coach had powerfully showed me the intensity of a father's love, and Mark's courage had saved my life. It was an unforgettable day!

When we returned to school for our junior year, Mark and I became leaders on the team. One of my most memorable college games came toward the end of our junior season. It was unique because it was being nationally televised! We were up by six points with just a minute to go. Our defense was on the field, determined to seal the victory.

The pressure mounted when their quarterback completed a couple of passes and got to our forty-yard line. It was a little too close for comfort. In order to avoid an embarrassing defeat, we had to tighten up our defense. Three plays later, it was fourth down and they needed a big play.

On the final play of the game, Mark broke through the center of the line and I came around from the side. We met on top of the quarterback! I made a lot of tackles throughout the years, but that one is still my favorite! I'll always remember it because it was one of the last tackles Mark and I made together.

As seniors, we got off to a good
start and won our first two games.
But then, during the week before
our third game, Mark got sick. At
first it was just a headache that
wouldn't go away. On Saturday,
Mark loaded up on aspirin and tried
to play, but by halftime his head
hurt too badly to continue.

I remember when I got back to
the dorm after the game, Mark was
already asleep even though it was
only six o'clock in the evening. I
tried to get him to call the doctor,
but he wouldn't.

During the next several weeks
there were days when he felt fine,
but there were others when he
didn't even make it out of bed. The
headaches just kept getting worse.
Finally the coaches insisted he see a

doctor and they called his parents.

When Coach and Nancy arrived on campus, it was pretty obvious they were worried about Mark. Because it was a university town, there were a number of excellent doctors around. They ended up visiting several specialists before receiving a definite diagnosis. The news was not good. Mark had a tumor in his brain!

I can't remember crying very many times in my life, but when Mark told me what was wrong, I sat on the bed in our dorm room and cried for a long time. Mark was the closest thing to a real brother I ever had. I couldn't imagine the grim prospect of losing him

Mark was the kind of friend who brought out the best in me. When he was on the field, I was a better player. When we were in the same class, I got better grades. There was something about having him around that challenged me to try harder and do better. When I heard the diagnosis, all of that seemed to come crashing down. Mark's college career and probably his dream to play pro football was over.

Several days later, Mark's doctor told him that the tumor needed to be surgically removed. From that moment on, Mark began to view the cancer that had invaded his body as if it were an opposing running back. He was unwilling to show it any mercy, and determined to stop its progress!

I'll never forget the chilly November day when Coach and

Nancy loaded Mark's stuff into their car to take him home. After a round of hugs, I waved goodbye and watched the Miller's car fade into the distance. It reminded me of the time when my dad left me when I was only seven years old. Again I felt the pain of being alone.

A little less than a week later, I received my first note from Mark. It was amazingly similar to the ones he had regularly received from his dad. Over the next few years, I would received a lot of notes from Mark. Each one was like a window into his soul and a source of strenth for me.

Most of all, Mark's notes revealed his enormous courage in the face of adversity. All of them touched me, and some of them touched me deeply. The first note read:

November 10, 1971

Alan,

You were right; it's going to take more than a couple of aspirin to cure my headaches! I just got back from seeing the cancer specialist and he confirmed that there is definitely a tumor in my brain. I guess that explains why I haven't been getting straight A's lately.

The doctor explained a lot more about cancer than I really care to know, but the bottom line is that I'm in for the toughest battle of my life. My dad likes to say that strength cannot be proven without pressure. I guess that I'm about to find out how strong I really am.

I heard that Saturday's game is on TV. You can count on me to be watching! Try to encourage Brad. He's going to be a good player; he just needs a little inspiration and confidence—just like you did several years ago.

Have a great week!

Mark

Brad was a sophomore and took Mark's position at middle linebacker. Mark was right. After some encouragement, Brad did become a good player. We dedicated the rest of the season to Mark. We lost only three games that year which was beyond our wildest dreams.

Christmas of 1971 was bittersweet because Mom was home alone, Mark was in the hospital recovering from surgery, and I was on the West Coast playing in a bowl game—the only one we made during my college career. It was a lot of fun, especially when we won by ten points. The obvious downside was that Mark wasn't there to enjoy it with us.

The best news that holiday season was the success of Mark's surgery: doctors removed a tumor the size of a golf ball. The bad news was they didn't think they had gotten all of it, so Mark began to undergo cancer treatments. Shortly after Mark began the treatments, I told him about my plans to get married.

Sally and I had met during our freshman year. After being friends for awhile, we started dating. She was beautiful, fun-loving, and studying to become an elementary school teacher. Not long after Sally and I announced our engagement, I received this note from Mark:

February 19, 1972

Alan,

I am happy to report that what little hair I had left after the surgery is now gone! It's pretty sad when my grandfather has more hair than I do. Actually, I am happy that my doctors seem to be encouraged by the treatments. Even though they make me sicker than a dog, they seem

*to be working. I don't know what
I'd do right now if I didn't have
Mom, Dad, and God to lean on!*

*Your phone call the other day
was great. I'm glad to hear that
you and Sally are now officially
engaged. I'll do everything I can
to be at the wedding. I'm praying
that you'll have a great marriage.*

*Congratulate Sally for me,
and I hope to see you soon!*

Mark

While Mark was going through
some of the most difficult experi-
ences imaginable, I was experiencing
some of the most exciting events of
my life. In the spring of 1972, Sally
and I were making wedding plans, I
was drafted to play professional foot-

ball, and I graduated with a
bachelor's degree in Business Admin-
istration. I called that time my
"triple crown."

Sally and I hoped that Mark
would be able to be the best man in
our wedding, but we weren't sure he
would be strong enough to do so.
The wedding was at the end of May
during a break in Mark's treatments, so he was there. Mark was
kind of embarrassed because he still
didn't have any hair, but I told him
he looked good bald, and besides,
maybe nobody would notice! Ev-
erybody noticed, but nobody cared.
More striking than Mark's hair loss
was his weight loss. He had always
been big, strong, and incredibly
muscular, but by the time of the
wedding, it seemed as if his skin

was collapsing around his bones. In spite of it all, he was a great best man.

After Sally and I got home from our honeymoon, I had to work harder than ever before in order to get into shape for my first training camp. In the midst of that time, I got the following note from Mark. He wrote it on Father's Day.

June 18, 1972

Alan,

I went out yesterday and bought my dad a Father's Day card. It's a nice card but it sure seems like an inadequate expression of appreciation in light of everything he has done for me! He is the one who saw potential in me long before anyone else did, and he is the one who inspired me to achieve far more than I ever could have dreamed.

I'm telling you this in order to say "thanks" for the way you constantly reminded me of what a good dad I have. Every time I was tempted to take him for granted, you reminded me how tough it was not to have a dad. Thanks for the encouragement!

I'm sure you won't be surprised when I tell you that he's still standing right beside me—with open arms—throughout every twist and turn of the past year. God gave me a great dad!

A grateful son,
Mark

About a month after getting Mark's note, I reported to training camp. It was exciting, but it quickly became apparent that playing professional football would not be easy. Though camp was challenging, that summer was still one of the brightest ones I can remember. Besides having wonderful weather, I made the team. The really bright spot was Mark's significant improvement. His doctors weren't willing to say that the cancer was in remission, but they were encouraged by his progress.

As Mark began to get a little of his strength back, I thought that having him come to some of our games would be a lot of fun. The coaches also thought it was a good idea, and so they gave Mark permission to watch the games from the sidelines. He made it to six games that season, and he even brought Coach along for a couple of them. It was just like old times. Following one of the games, I got a note that Mark wrote on the Monday morning after he got home.

October 16, 1972

Alan,

 Thanks again for inviting Dad and me to the game. From the time I was a little kid, I dreamed of standing on the sidelines during a pro football game. Of course I wanted to be a player instead of merely being a spectator. I have to confess that it wasn't easy to be so close and yet so far from my lifelong dream.

Funny thing about dreams: they are sometimes hard to find, but even harder to fulfill. On our way home, I decided that it's time for me to find a new dream. I'm going to finish my degree, and maybe give teaching a shot.

Thanks again for letting me come to the game, and don't stop chasing your dream!

Mark

The next summer, Mark finished his Bachelor's degree in Education and since he was continuing to feel good, he started to work part time at the high school—helping his dad with the football team and teaching one class. It was a sort of trial run to see if he had the strength to do it.

That fall, I made arrangements again for Mark to come to my games. He was too tired to come to the first one, but he and Coach did make it to the second game of our season. That was an important day because after the game, Sally and I took them to dinner and told them that we were expecting our first child. They were extremely happy for us. It was like telling Coach that he was going to become a grandfather. A few days later I received this from Mark:

September 25, 1973

Alan,
*   You're a defensive end because you were never very good at hold-*

ing onto a football, and so I'm a little worried about you holding a baby. Try not to fumble! Seriously, I'm thrilled for you and Sally. I'll pray that Sally will be healthy throughout the pregnancy. And if you need any advice, call my dad. He's been through it all!

By the way, if you need a boy's name, I think "Mark" has kind of a nice ring to it!

Congratulations,
Mark

Mark didn't make it to either of our next two games. He said he was busy and tired, but I soon found out it was more than that. About a month after we had told Mark about the baby, I got a call from

Coach. Mark was back in the hospital. The cancer had returned.

Mark was in and out of the hospital throughout the rest of our season. They started the treatments again, and he kept getting weaker and weaker and weaker. I tried to occasionally call and encourage him, but it was becoming increasingly clear that the treatments were not working very well.

I knew that things weren't looking very good when the notes stopped arriving in the mail. I made a quick trip back to Detroit to see him right after the season was over. He was pretty low. He had lost even more weight, and barely looked like the Mark with whom I'd grown up and played football. Coach told me that the doctors had found cancer in other areas of his body. Hope was beginning to fade.

It was probably about a month later, while I was at home asleep, that the phone rang in the middle of the night. It was Coach. They had just taken Mark to the intensive care area. It didn't look good. Sally and I left at about 5 A.M. and made it to the hospital by early afternoon.

The nurses let us see Mark for only short periods of time. Even then, he was so heavily medicated that I don't think he knew we were there. As we stood at Mark's bedside, Coach handed me an envelope. Mark had written me a note a few days earlier and he wanted to make sure I got it. Here's what it said:

April 21, 1974

Alan,

I'm not feeling very good today. It's pretty obvious that the treatments aren't working. I've been in the hospital for eight days now, and I'm beginning to wonder if the next time I go home, instead of going to 1631 Western Drive, I'll be going to heaven.

I don't think anybody expects to die at my age, but I have to admit I've had a pretty good life. I've got a great family, wonderful friends, and a place in heaven that must be about ready for me to move into. Mom and Dad are doing a lot of crying these days, but at least we all know we're not going to say

"Goodbye," just "See you later."
Alan, I know how badly you
always wanted a father. As I've
tried to tell you many times, there
is a Father in heaven that I'm
probably going to see pretty soon.
Please let God be your Father, so
I can see you there too!

Your brother,
Mark

That was the first time Mark had
ever signed one of his notes that
way. It was also one his most direct
in terms of spiritual encouragement.
Mark was as close to me as any
brother could be, and while I didn't
envy his physical circumstances, I
wanted the peace that characterized
Mark's life. There was something in

his soul that wasn't in mine.

I couldn't imagine how angry and bitter I would have been if it were me in his situation. Clearly, Mark's faith in God had made an unmistakable difference in his life.

Mark and Coach had both told me about God on numerous occasions, but I never wanted to listen. I always thought they were trying to convince me to become religious— something I had no desire to become. I'd met several people along the way who loudly talked about God, but who didn't seem to act very godly. Coach and Mark, however, were different. They had a way of living their beliefs in quiet, yet powerful ways.

After reading Mark's note, and with a growing desire in my heart for the kind of peace Mark had, I did what I had done on so many other occasions—I asked Coach for help. He suggested we go for a ride, so we climbed into his pickup truck and drove toward our old high school. Coach pulled up to the football stadium where I hadn't been for several years. It was fairly late in the evening and nobody was there. Coach used his key to open the gate, and we walked in. After he turned on a few small lights, we walked out onto the field. As we talked, Coach told me that it was impossible for him to step onto that field without seeing Mark in his mind. Mark was Coach's only son. It was obvious that from the moment of Mark's birth, the two of them had prized the time they the time they spent together.

After he talked a little bit about his memories, Coach began to tell me the story of another father who also deeply loved his son. Like Coach, this father also had just one very special son who possessed a rare combination of capability, compassion, and courage. Like Coach and Mark's relationship with me, this father and his son also demonstrated their love in order to bring hope to the fatherless. The father whom Coach told me about wasn't just anybody; He was God—the greatest Father who ever lived!

As Coach talked, I heard God's story in a way that I had never heard it before. This time it didn't go in one ear and out the other—it actually landed in my heart. What I heard Coach tell me that evening was that God's story wasn't about church services or stained glass, but that God's story is a family's story about a Father's love, a Son's courage, and the bright hope that they offer to the world.

Coach made it very clear that God's desire wasn't to turn me into a religious person, but to bring me into His family. He wants us to become His children, and He wants to be our father. Coach found a football under one of the benches, and while tossing it to me, he asked, "Do you remember the very first time we met?"

As I tried to remember, Coach reminded me that it was at their house, just a few weeks after Mark and I met in the seventh grade. The only thing

Coach knew about me at the time was that my parents were divorced, and that I didn't have a father. Coach said when he saw Mark and me playing in the backyard that afternoon, he wasn't watching a potential football player, but a kid without a dad. He said he and Nancy noticed how lonely I was, prompting them to encourage Mark to invite me over to their house as often as he wanted. Coach recalled that he could still remember saying, "I can't think of a better cure for loneliness than our house." And he was right—their house was always filled with people, food, and lots of noise. I loved every minute of it.

Coach then said, "Alan, when God the Father looks at you through heaven's window, He sees you the same way I saw you back in 1962. Sure, you're older and bigger than you were back then, but what you still need more than anything else is a father. I don't know why your dad left, but I'm sure that it was devastating. One thing about the greatest Father is that He will *never* walk away from any of His children. Unlike the Father, all of us have chosen to walk in the direction of our own desires instead of in the direction of God's will."

Coach went on to remind me how he had encouraged Mark to reach out to me and become my friend. Similarly, God the Father encouraged His only Son, Jesus, to also reach out and seek to become the friend of every man, woman, and child, because all of us are spiritually lonely and fatherless. Our greatest need in life is to come home to the family of God.

I had to admit to Coach that Mark had devoted enormous energy into becoming my friend. He gave of his time; he introduced me to his parents; he showed me a family that loved God and each other. I can't begin to count the number of sacrifices Mark made in order to help me to see the love of God and experience the warmth of a family.

Coach explained that in order for Jesus to reach me, it required an effort far greater than Mark's.

Jesus left the comforts of His home in heaven in order to come into our neighborhood. The neighborhood of Earth was far different from heaven, not to mention far more dangerous because sin was everywhere.

One of the ways Jesus dealt with the risks He faced was to maintain a close relationship with His Father. When Jesus was about 12 years old, while on a family trip, His mom and step-dad noticed He was missing. Unlike most boys His age, He hadn't gotten into mischief. He was at the Temple. When they found Him, Jesus seemed surprised that they didn't understand His desire to be "in His Father's House." Like Mark, Jesus loved spending time with His Father!

As Jesus grew older, the pressures that confronted Him grew stronger. When He was about thirty years old, He spent forty days and nights in a wilderness withstanding the fiercest time of temptation imaginable.

Coach said, "I can't imagine how His Father must have felt when Jesus went into that wilderness!"

Coach wondered whether or not it might have been a little bit like the time that Mark left home to go to college. In the late '60s and early '70s, many university campuses were fairly similar to a spiritual wilderness.

Coach and Nancy knew that Mark would be presented with a wide array of temptations, yet they believed that he had the spiritual courage to withstand them. They also wanted him to continue to reach out to me.

Coach also told me that when Jesus went through His time of temptation, His Father's Word inspired Him to overcome the pressure to sin. It was because of that example that Coach started writing notes to Mark.

Referring to the notes, Coach said, "I know they weren't as powerful as God's Word, but I hoped they would encourage him to spiritually succeed."

In spite of the temptation, Jesus perfectly followed His Father's voice and was faithful to His Father's values. As for Mark, while he wasn't perfect, he did a good job of living up to his father's values as well. Mark wasn't loud about his faith, but the way he lived his faith spoke more clearly than words ever could.

After Jesus had successfully navigated His way through the temptations, He began to passionately seek and befriend the spiritually fatherless.

Jesus met people with horrible diseases. He met those constrained by poverty. And He met many others who were plagued with the painful memories and consequences of past failure. The common thread connecting them was the fact that they were all spiritual orphans who needed a Father. Because of their need, everytime Jesus met someone, He shared His Father's Word and showed His Father's love.

As Jesus demonstrated His Father's compassion, He offered a fresh brand of hope that people had never experienced before. It was an opportunity to become part of an eternal family—a family where love is freely dispensed, where hurts are properly healed, and where hope never dies.

Tragically, only a few accepted His offer of hope. Jesus gathered together a small group of brothers and sisters, but most refused to listen to Him.

Coach reminded me that just as sin had caused the people of Jesus' day to reject His offer of hope, sin had also led me to resist their repeated efforts to tell me about God.

In spite of the rejection, Jesus continued to pursue His "game plan" to defeat the sin that had for so long separated us from His Father. In order to accomplish that, it required Jesus to demonstrate the most extraordinary courage imaginable.

Coach told me that one of Mark's prayers was for God to do "whatever it takes" in order to reach into my heart. What none of us realized was that the "whatever it takes" would turn out to be cancer. For some reason while life was peaceful and ordinary I didn't want to think about the deep issues of the heart. But through Mark's suffering—and demonstration of grace under pressure—my heart softened and finally opened. I wish that I would have listened earlier. I wish that I wouldn't have been so stubborn. I wish that it wouldn't have cost Mark so much.

For Jesus, when He courageously told His Father that He was willing to do whatever it takes to reach the hearts of people, His "whatever it takes" was not cancer, but a cross. As growing numbers of people rejected His offer of hope, the tide of public opinion turned violently against Jesus. It all culminated one night when He was arrested on a series of false charges.

In a mockery of a trial, Jesus was convicted of crimes He did not commit and was sentenced to die. After being brutally beaten, He was taken to a barren spot just outside the city of Jerusalem where He was nailed to a cross. As He hung there dying, the entire world turned black as a mark of His Father's grief. Within a matter of hours, Jesus was dead. The very ones the Father had invited to become His children had killed His only Son!

On the evening of His death, Jesus' body was taken down from the cross and placed in a borrowed tomb. In the wake of His death, Jesus' small family of followers began to wonder whether or not the promise to become a part of God's family had been broken. What no one understood at the time was that Jesus would not remain in the tomb.

In a twist of events unparalleled in history, just three days after his death, Jesus came out of the tomb—very much alive. He had overcome the forces of sin and death, and destroyed the barrier that had kept us out of God's family!

The Son's courage on the cross, inspired by the Father's love, had brought bright new hope to the world. That was something that only God could do.

Coach had a little Bible in his pocket. He pulled it out and read me a verse that I had heard before, but that I needed to hear again. It said,

"For God so loved the world, that

He gave his only begotten Son, that whosoever believeth in Him should not perish, but have everlasting life" (John 3:16).

Coach explained that just as I had entered my human family through the physical process of birth, I could enter the family of God through faith in Jesus Christ alone.

At that point in our conversation, Coach didn't need to persuade or convince me any further that I needed to believe in Jesus. I was not only ready, but eager to become a child of the Greatest Father Who Ever Lived!

On the 40-yard line in that empty high school football stadium, I got down on my knees and asked God to forgive me of my sins, to make me one of His children, and to give me the gift of eternal life—a home in heaven.

After I prayed my simple prayer, Coach gave me one of the biggest hugs that I can ever remember. I thanked him for being such a great example. I asked him if he'd keep helping me and be my coach in my new relationship with God. He quickly agreed.

We talked for a few more minutes, then returned to Coach's house, where I wanted to tell Sally what had happened.

When we got there, Sally and I walked out to the backyard in order to talk. She was overjoyed when she heard what I had done. I knew that she would be happy because about six months earlier, while attending a Bible study with the wives of several

of my teammates, she had also become a child of God. Beginning that
night, Sally and I were bonded together as we had never been before.

Sally and I had an awfully hard
time getting to sleep that night. We
had the longest talk we had had in
a very long time. We talked about
our new relationship with God,
about our marriage, about becoming parents—and about Mark. I ad-
mitted that I had made a lot of mistakes in my life, but that with my
new Father's direction, I was ready
for a fresh start.

Two days after my life-changing
choice, while Sally and I gathered
with Mark's family around his hospital bed, Mark died. I can still remember the time: 2:47 P.M. When
the doctor told us he was gone,

Coach wrapped his arms around Mark's very thin body and told him goodbye. It reminded me of the time when Coach pulled Mark out of Lake Michigan and into the sailboat. It was one more powerful reminder of the depth of their love.

After the doctor left the room, we huddled together, our arms around each other, sobbing and not really knowing what to say or do next. I finally broke the silence and quietly said,

"I'll see you later, big brother."

Mark died on a Wednesday and his funeral was on Friday morning. It was one of the most difficult events I have ever attended. The church where it was held was packed with people. Many of our friends from high school and college attended.

Most of the coaching staff from college was also there. Even though Mark was still a very young man, he had touched many lives, and I was at the top of that list.

During the funeral, I was struck by Coach's strength when he spoke about Mark. His voice became very soft when he said,

"Even though I am extremely sad today, I also know that Mark is finally Home. We gave him a home to live in for the 24 years that he was with us. Now, God the Father has given him a Home to live in for all of eternity."

He then read this verse to the audience,

" *'In My Father's house are many mansions: I go to prepare a place for you. And if I go and prepare a place for*

*you, I will come again, and receive you
unto Myself; that where I am, there you
may be also' (John 14:1–3)."*

Coach finished by saying, "Enjoy
your new Home, Mark. We'll be together again someday!"

Not surprisingly, there wasn't a
dry eye in the room.

The day after the funeral, Sally
and I traveled home. It was hard to
jump back into the routine of life,
but with a baby on the way and training camp just around the corner, we
didn't have much of a choice. It was
just three weeks later when Sally went
into the hospital. After several hours
of labor, our 7-pound, 15-ounce mas-
terpiece was born. As we looked at
his perfectly formed little body, Sally
and I both sensed that our baby boy
was not simply our dream come true,

but that he was also a wonderful gift from God Himself. We named him "Mark Alan."

As I began my adventure in fatherhood, I frequently called Coach for advice, and I also began to listen to what the Greatest Father Who Ever Lived had to say! Mark had given me a Bible for a college graduation gift. As I began to read it, I heard the inspiring voice of my Father directing me, just as Coach had done on so many occasions. At about that same time, I also made another commitment—to share my heart and life with my new son. I wanted to show Mark Alan my love. I wanted to inspire him to withstand every pressure that he would face. I wanted to encourage him to fulfill his ultimate potential. Based on those desires—when Mark was just one day old—I wrote him the first of what would become literally hundreds of notes. My first one read:

5:45 A.M.
Tuesday, May 28

Mark,
*   I have endured a lot and enjoyed a lot in my life, but your birth yesterday was the most exciting day I've ever had! It was a lot better than the bowl game that I played in, and I can't imagine the Super Bowl being any better.*
*   Even though I am a rookie at fatherhood, I'll try to be the best dad that I can be. As we begin this adventure together, this is my commitment to you:*

I will always love you. While I was growing up, I didn't experience love from my father. My mom did her best, but I always wanted a dad. I promise that we'll spend time together and talk together. I would like not only to be your dad, but someday, your friend as well. I love you!

I will try my best to inspire you to achieve great things. My life would probably be in shambles today if it were not for the coaches and friends who inspired me to follow my dreams. I'd like to teach you to make good choices, lead you away from mistakes, and encourage you to develop your talents and gifts.

I will also try my best to always give you hope. I can't pre-

dict what pain or problems you will experience through the course of your life, but I promise to stand with you and show you that regardless of how tough life may become, there is hope for a brighter and better tomorrow.

Mark, I met you only yesterday, but I'm already proud to call you "my son."

Love,
Dad

WHEN I READ Alan's story, it took me back to that unforgettable day when I first heard it, flying from Seattle to Phoenix. I can still remember being surprised by the pilot's announcement that the plane was descending for a landing. I just couldn't believe that Alan and I had been talking for so long.

Jenny had been a follower of Jesus Christ for a long time, and I had gone to church with her on several occasions, but for some reason it had never really connected with me. The topics of "God" and "faith" didn't seem very relevant to the issues and concerns of my life. During that season of my life, I was more concerned about promotions at work, low scores on the golf course, and more money in the bank.

However, after listening to Alan tell me about the transformation that had occurred in his life, I had to admit that God's story was beginning to make more sense to me than ever before. As we walked into the airport terminal, Jenny was waiting for me. Also waiting was Alan's son, Mark. Alan introduced me to Mark, and I introduced them to Jenny. Mark worked with his dad in a very successful insurance agency, and it was quickly apparent to see that they were not just father and son, but friends as well!

As we walked together toward the baggage claim area, Alan asked if he could call me sometime in order to talk more about life and fatherhood. I said, "Sure." I gave him my business card, picked up my suitcase, and headed home.

Over the next several weeks, Alan and I had lunch on several occasions. Every time we talked, I had a

different excuse for why I didn't see
the need to commit my life to God.
With each passing day, Alan's words
and contagious spirit weighed more
heavily upon my heart. I spent several nearly sleepless nights, tossing
and turning, unable to stop thinking
about our conversations. I kept won-
dering whether Alan had been telling me about what had worked for
him, or what *I really needed.*

Finally, late one night, with
Jenny sound asleep, I got up and
decided that I needed to settle
things between God and me. I *did*
need a heavenly Father before I became a father. After I found the
Bible Alan had given to me, I read
the verses he had marked in it. One
was John 3:16—

"For God so loved the world that He

*gave his only begotten Son, that whoso-
ever believeth in Him should not perish,
but have everlasting life."*

Another was John 1:12—

*"But as many as received Him, to
them he gave the power to become the
sons of God, even to them that believe
on his name."*

Deciding that I didn't want to
wait any longer, I walked down the
hallway into the bedroom that
would soon become our nursery.

I bowed down next to the crib and
asked God to forgive me of my sin
and bring me into His family. It was
an incredibly emotional moment as I
received the Father's love by believing
in His Son, Jesus Christ, as my Savior.
In that room decorated for a baby, I
became a new baby myself, a child in
the arms of God, a son of the Greatest

Father Who Ever Lived.

As I was talking to my new Father, Jenny woke up and heard me. Even though it was nearly midnight, she came in to find out what was going on. She was so excited for me and for our family. After praying together, we went back to bed. For the first time in a long time, I slept like a baby that night!

It's hard to believe that it's been nearly two years since all of that happened. Zachary was born just a month after I made my momentous choice to follow Jesus. Alan and Sally have continued to be extremely kind to Jenny and me. They lead a Bible study that we regularly attend. Alan has become a great example to follow. He's shown me how to be the kind of husband and father that I need to be.

I decided to finish writing this to-
night after playing an incredible
round of golf. It was a great round
not because of my score, but because
of the other three players that made
up our foursome: Alan, his son Mark,
and "Coach." Coach has been visiting Alan and Sally from Detroit. He
is an amazing man, whose influence
is now reaching a third generation.

In light of all that's happened,
I'll always be thankful for that foggy
Seattle morning when a long and
frustrating delay led me to meet
the Greatest Father Who Ever Lived.

> *"See how great a love the
> Father has bestowed upon
> us, that we should be
> called children of God"*
>   *(1 John 3:2).*

If you are a father, consider writing your son or daughter a note that expresses your love and commitment to him or her.

Dear

_____

_____

_____

_____

_____

_____

_____

Love,

Dear

_____

_____

_____

_____

_____

_____

_____

_____

Love,

Dad

HOW TO BECOME A CHRISTIAN

THE BIBLE DESCRIBES three key steps in becoming a Christian. I MUST:

1 ADMIT that I am a sinner, unable to live up to God's standard of perfection and, therefore, deserving of eternal separation from God.

"For all have sinned, and come short of the glory of the God" (Romans 3:23).

"For the wages of sin is death; but the gift of God is eternal life through Jesus Christ our Lord" (Romans 6:23).

ACKNOWLEDGE that Jesus is God's only Son who died on the cross to pay the penalty for my sin. He arose from the grave three days later in victory over death.

"But God commendeth his love toward us in that, while we were yet sinners, Christ died for us" (Romans 5:8).

"Christ died for our sins according to the scriptures; and that he was was buried, and that he rose again the third day, according to the scriptures" (1 Corinthians 15:3, 4).

BELIEVE in Jesus Christ alone for the forgiveness of my sins and the gift of eternal life in heaven.

"For God so loved the world, that he gave his only begotten Son, that whosoever believeth in him should not perish, but have everlasting life"
(John 3:16).

"For whosoever shall call upon the name of the Lord shall be saved"
(Romans 10:13).

❖   ❖   ❖

IF YOU ARE READY to become a Christian, honestly believing each of the statements above to be true, then pray from your heart the following prayer:

"God in Heaven, I know that I am a sinner, and I understand that my sin deserves to be severely punished. But because of your love, Jesus took my punishment when He died on the cross. Please forgive me of my sin and give me the gift of eternal life. Thank you for hearing my prayer and receiving me into your family.

Amen."

WELCOME to God's family!
Please quickly contact a trusted
Christian friend or church, and tell
them about your belief in Christ.

P.O. Box 882 • Kokomo, IN 46903-0882

ABOUT THE AUTHOR
DANIEL JOHNSON has pastored local
churches in Illinois and Indiana. He currently
ministers in Kokomo, Indiana, where he re-
sides with his wife, Linda, and their four
children.

ARE THESE PROVIDENCE PUBLICATIONS IN YOUR LIBRARY?

THE GREATEST SOLDIER WHO EVER LIVED

This is a story of liberation told in a fresh, new way. *The Greatest Soldier Who Ever Lived* is a poignant and powerful parable of family, faith, and freedom. It will undoubtedly touch your heart. And it may even change your life—forever!

THE TEACHER'S DAILY HELPER

This year-long devotional guide is structured around 52 teaching themes. *The Teacher's Daily Helper* is designed so that in two to five minutes a day, through the disciplines of prayer and meditation, a teacher will be encouraged to focus on God.

THE
GREATEST
SOLDIER
WHO EVER
LIVED

DANIEL R. JOHNSON

The
TEACHER'S
Daily
HELPER
A Year's Treasury of
Topical Meditations

JON W. TICE

ORDERING
INFORMATION

To order additional copies of
The Greatest Father Who Ever Lived,
please contact
Providence Publications toll-free at

1-877-408-7038

WEB SITE:
www.providencepubl.com

MAILING ADDRESS:
P.O. Box 882
Kokomo, IN 46903-0882